Let's Find Out About SNAKES

LET'S FIND OUT ABOUT
SNAKES

by MARTHA and CHARLES SHAPP

Pictures by René Martin

Franklin Watts, Inc.
575 Lexington Avenue
New York, N.Y. 10022

SBN 531-00043-5
Library of Congress Catalog Card Number: 68-19238
Copyright © 1968 by Franklin Watts, Inc.
Printed in the United States of America
by The Moffa Press, Inc.

6

Let's Find Out About SNAKES

Snakes are very strange animals.
Snakes have no legs or feet.
But snakes can crawl,

Black snake

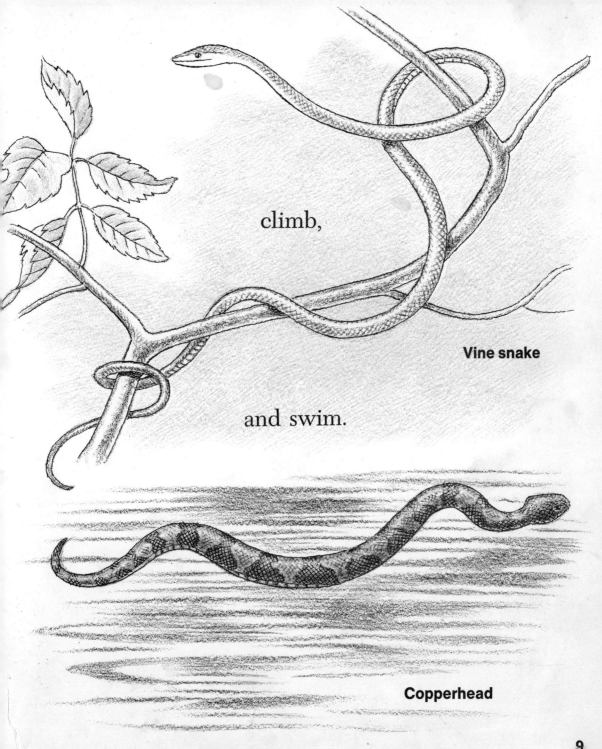

climb,

Vine snake

and swim.

Copperhead

A snake has no outside ear openings.
It cannot hear in the ordinary way.
But it can "feel" you coming.
As you walk, your feet shake the ground a
little.
Snakes can feel the lightest shaking of the
ground.

Bull snake

A snake has no movable eyelids.
Its eyes are always open.
A snake sleeps with its eyes open.

Grass snake

Western racer

A snake uses its tongue to smell with.
Its two-pointed tongue shoots in and out
   "smelling" the air.
That is how a snake knows that a friend or
   an enemy or food is near.

Rattlesnake

Mud snake

Snakes are reptiles.
All reptiles have skins covered with scales.

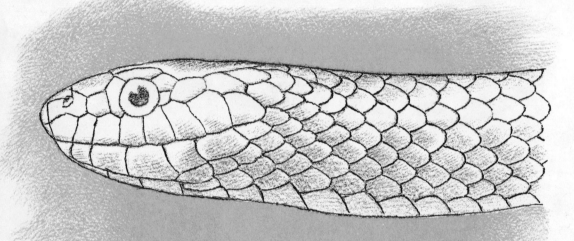

SMOOTH SCALES

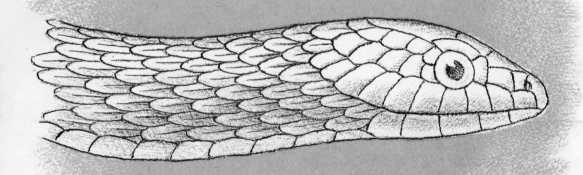

KEELED SCALES

OTHER REPTILES

LIZARD

CROCODILE

Many snakes are beautiful.
Their skins are brightly colored, with
interesting designs on them.

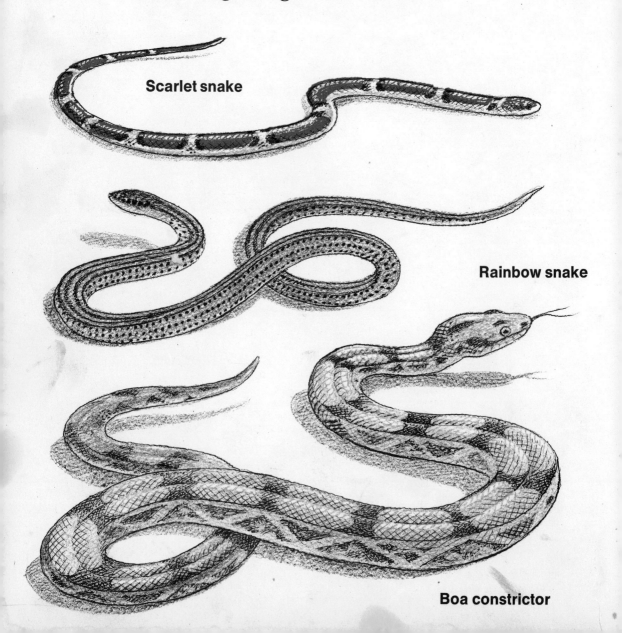

Scarlet snake

Rainbow snake

Boa constrictor

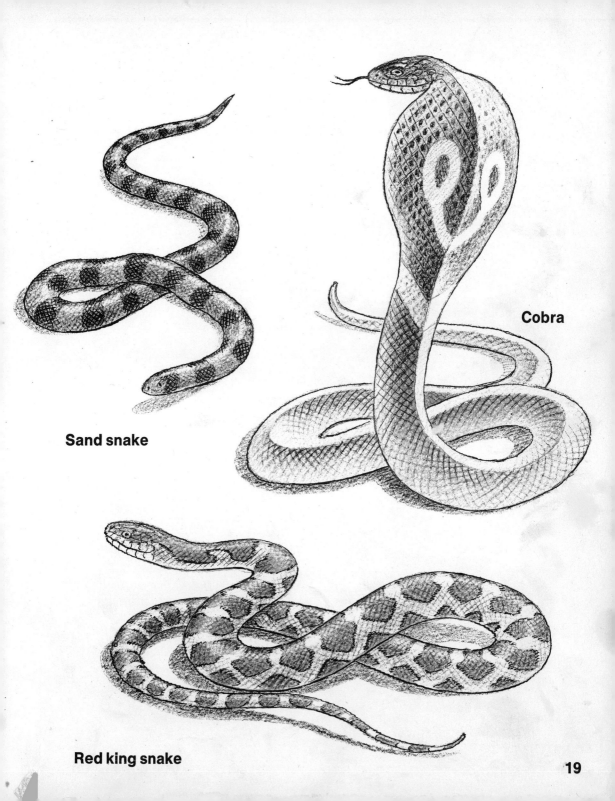

Sand snake

Cobra

Red king snake

19

A snake can change its skin.
Several times during its life, a snake crawls
out of its old skin and comes out with a
bright shiny new skin.

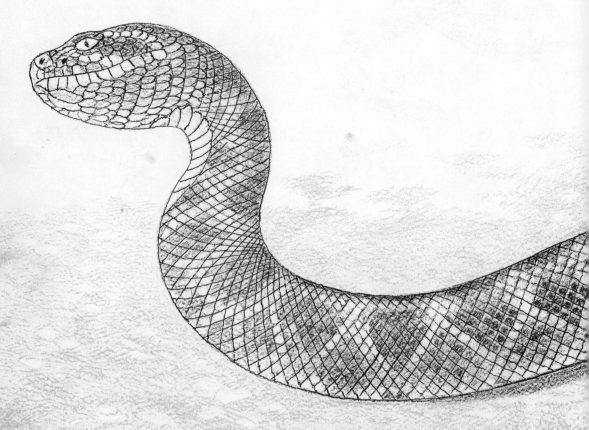

Rattlesnake

There are snakes of all sizes.
Some are as short as ten inches.

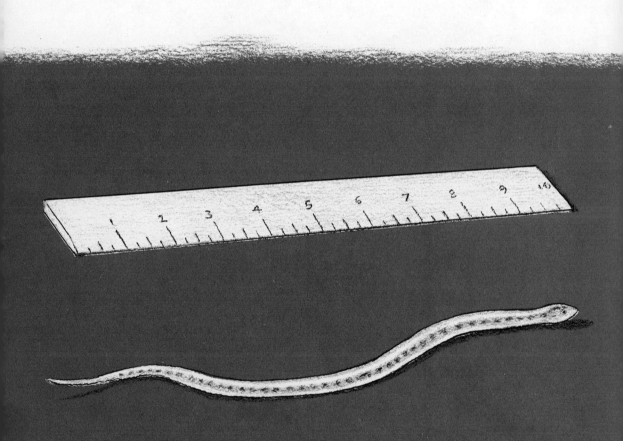

DeKay's snake

Other snakes are as long as thirty feet.

Anaconda

Scarlet king snake

Snakes cannot keep themselves warm.
They get their heat by lying in the sun on
warm rocks or soil.
That is why most snakes live in warm
climates.

Those snakes that live in cold climates must
   go underground in the winter.
They stay underground until the warm
   spring comes.

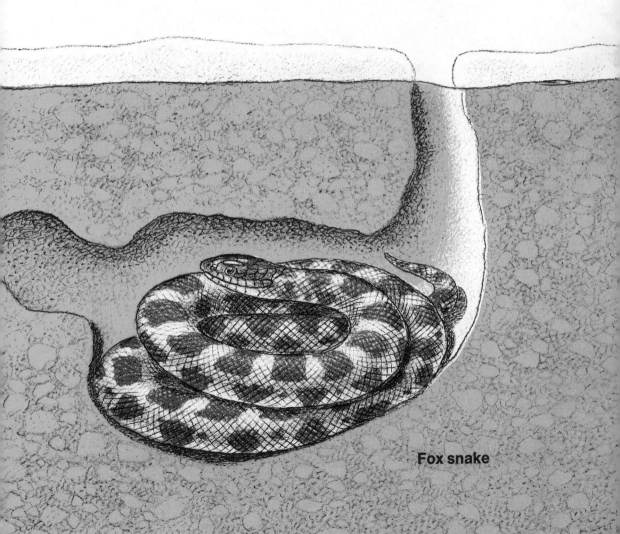

Fox snake

Most snakes live on the ground.
But there are some kinds of snakes that live
  in trees.
Tree snakes are good climbers.

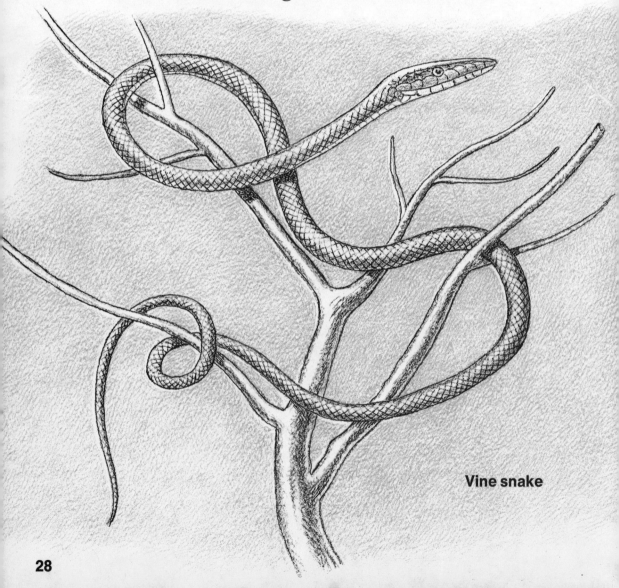

Vine snake

Rough green snake

Other snakes live in the water.
They are very good swimmers.
But they cannot breathe underwater as
    fishes do.

Common water snake

Water snakes must come up out of the water to breathe air.

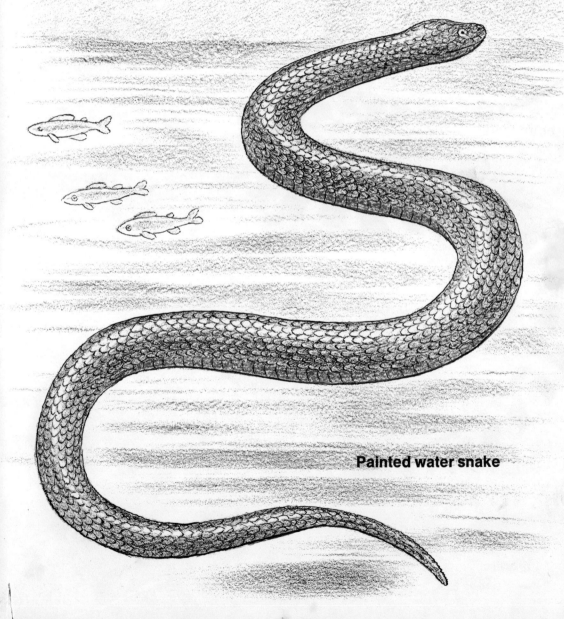

Painted water snake

Snakes eat many different things.

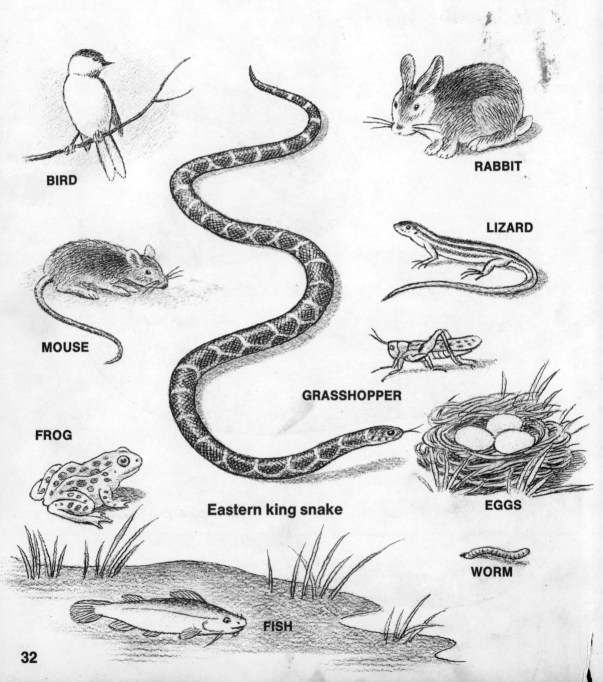

BIRD

RABBIT

MOUSE

LIZARD

GRASSHOPPER

FROG

Eastern king snake

EGGS

WORM

FISH

On farms, snakes eat the small animals that eat the farmers' crops.

RAT

Corn snake

33

A snake swallows its food whole.
After it swallows an animal, you can see a
  big bulge in the snake's body.
After such a big meal, a snake can go
  without food for a few weeks.

Whip snake

Prairie rattlesnake

Some snakes eat other snakes.
The king snake kills and eats rattlesnakes.
The rattler's poison does not hurt the king
snake.

California king snake

Snakes have enemies.
Snakes are killed and eaten by other animals.

WEASEL

OWL

SKUNK

HAWK

Most snakes are hatched from eggs.

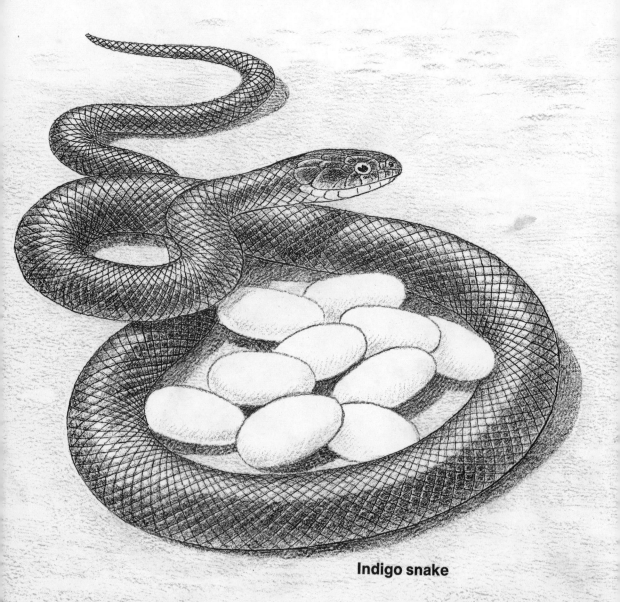

Indigo snake

But some kinds of snakes give birth to live
  baby snakes.
All baby snakes can take care of themselves
  right after they are hatched or born.

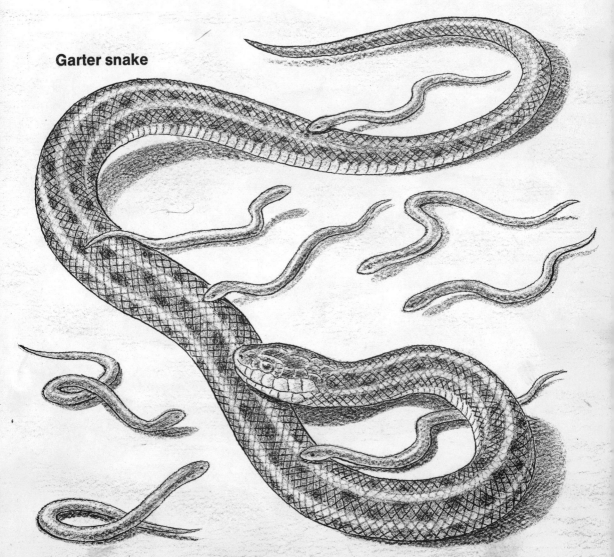

Garter snake

Harmless snakes

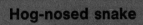
Hog-nosed snake

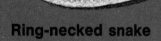
Ring-necked snake

Rosy boa

42

Most snakes are harmless.
But there are some poisonous snakes.
Find out what poisonous snakes live in your
part of the country.
You can find out at a zoo, or at a
museum, or from books.
Learn to recognize these snakes and **keep
away from them.**

Sidewinder

The rattlesnake is a poisonous snake that is
found in many places.
It has a rattle on the end of its tail.
When a rattlesnake gets angry or frightened,
it shakes its tail and makes a rattling noise.

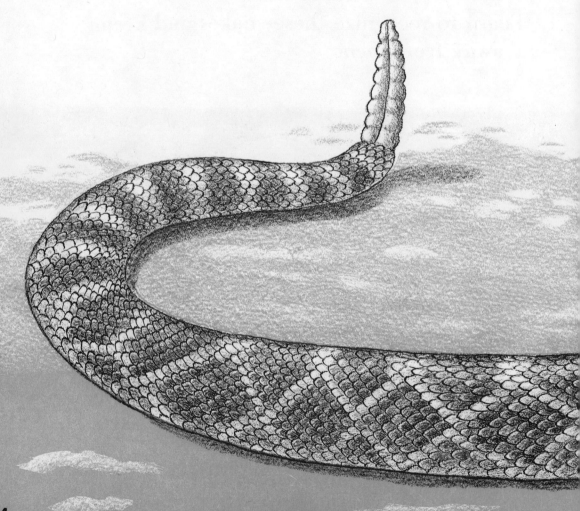

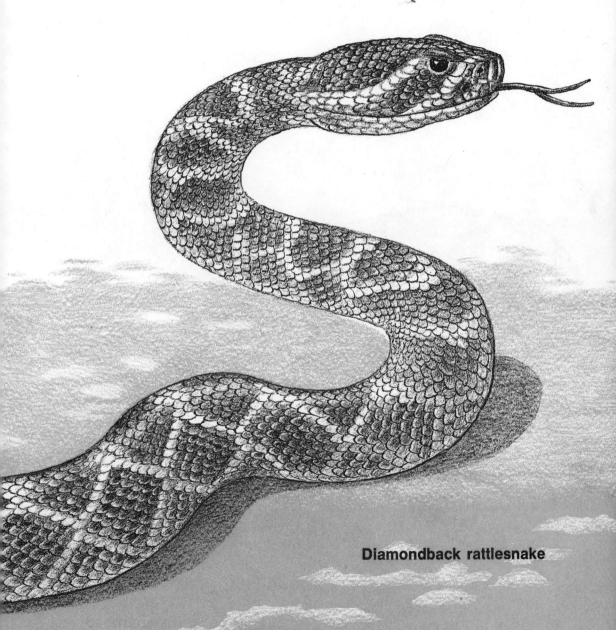

Diamondback rattlesnake

The copperhead is a dangerous snake.
Its head is a red-brown like copper.

Copperhead

The water moccasin is another dangerous
snake.
It is dark brown and lives in swamps.

Water moccasin

Poisonous snakes have two long sharp teeth
  called fangs.
Inside these fangs are canals.
When poisonous snakes bite, the poison
  comes down through these canals.

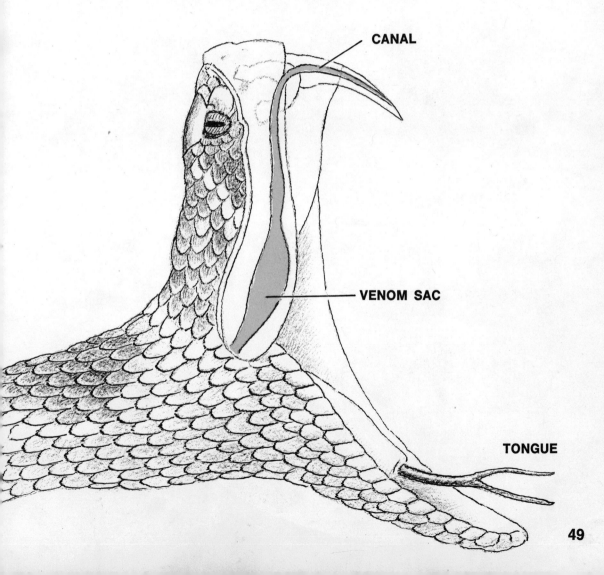

CANAL

VENOM SAC

TONGUE

One of the most poisonous of American snakes is the coral snake.
Fortunately for us, the coral snake is very shy and lives underground most of the time.

Coral snake

If there are poisonous snakes where you live,
be careful when you walk in deep grass,
when you climb trees, or when you are
near rocks.
Wear gloves and keep your legs covered.
Make some noise as you walk.
This warns a snake that someone is coming
and it will get out of your way.

Snakes are very interesting animals.
Most of them are harmless.
But when you are near them, remember
   your ABC's.

Red diamond rattlesnakes

Always

Be

Careful

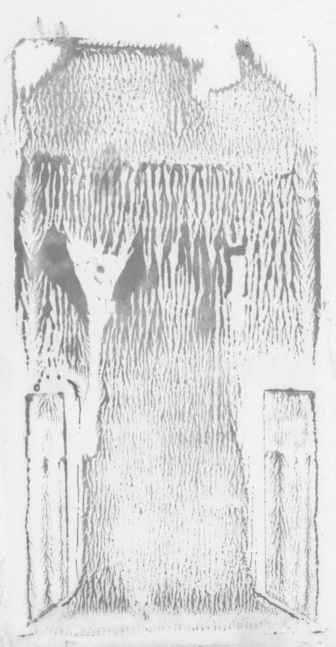